Zacharias Tanee Fomum

# GOD'S LOVE AND FORGIVENESS

# GOD'S LOVE AND FORGIVENESS

By
ZACHARIAS TANEE FOMUM
© 1976, Z.T. FOMUM

Published by

CHRISTIAN
PUBLISHING
HOUSE

cph@ztfministry.org
www.ztfbooks.com
www. ztfministry.org

All Rights Reserved

Unless otherwise stated, the Scripture quotations in this book are from the Revised Standard Version of the Holy Bible, the British Edition.

In grateful memory of my father
SOLOMON FOMUM TANEE
in whose life I first saw Jesus

# TABLE OF CONTENTS

1. **IN THE BEGINNING**
    God's Perfect Creation
    Man In God's Image And Likeness
    Fellowship Between God And Man

2. **SIN AND ITS RESULTS**
    Adam's Sin
    The Results Of Adam's Sin
    All Have Sinned
    Sin In Practice
    The Wages Of Sin
    Human Attempts At Reaching God

3. **THE LOVE OF GOD**
    God's Love For The Sinner
    God's Love Revealed In Christ
    Jesus Christ And His Mission
    How Jesus Did It
    Why Jesus Did It: Love
    A Risen Christ: God's Seal On The Work On The Cross
    Benefits From Christ's Death And Resurrection

4. **GOD FORGIVES YOU**
    What You Must Do
    A Time For Action
    Receiving Christ

5. **BECAUSE YOU ARE FORGIVEN**
    Eternal Life
    Eternal Security
    Heavenly Citizenship
    Tell Others
    Pray Every Day
    Read The Bible Every Day
    Finally

Chapter 1

# IN THE BEGINNING

GOD'S LOVE AND FORGIVENESS

## GOD'S PERFECT CREATION

The Bible tells us that God created the world and everything in it, including the sun, the moon, sea animals and land animals... When this was done, *"God saw that it was good"* (Genesis 1:25). God also *"created man in his own image, in the image of God he created him; male and female he created them"* (Genesis 1:27). After everything was created, both man and animal, land and sea... *"God saw everything that he had made, and behold, it was very good"* (Genesis 1:31). If God saw something and said that it was very good, it must have been perfect in every sense. Man was, therefore, perfect at creation. There was nothing imperfect in him. He was such that when God looked at him, God's heart was glad and He could say something like this: "This is My perfect and wonderful creature."

## MAN IN GOD'S IMAGE AND LIKENESS

The creation of man in the image and likeness of God was something special to man. The other creatures did not share this nature. God had a special purpose for creating man that way. The purpose was, first of all, that man should be specially related to Him: being able to understand Him, talk with Him, enjoy Him, and glorify Him for ever. Secondly, it was that man should take charge of the rest of creation: controlling it and directing it.

The special relationship between God and man was meant to please God and man. God wanted it and man needed it. Although

God wanted it, He could do without it. Man, however, needed it if he was to function properly.

## FELLOWSHIP BETWEEN GOD AND MAN

God actually did come down to man to talk with him (Genesis 3:8). Probably, during these conversations, man (Adam and Eve) told God that he loved Him and that he was very grateful to Him for creating him, and giving him such a beautiful life and garden. He probably told Him that he would love and obey Him all the time and do everything He asked him to do. These special meetings between God and man must have been wonderful.

MAN  GOD

*Everything was so wonderful. Each must have felt at home in the presence of the other and when they talked. There was no barrier between them.*

## QUESTIONS

1. How did God see man from the beginning?
2. How did God see the rest of the creation from the beginning?
3. What is the first reason why God created man (in the image and likeness of God)?
4. What kind of relationship existed between God and man at the beginning?

Chapter 2

# SIN AND ITS RESULTS

## ADAM'S SIN

For the relationship between God and man to continue without any barrier, God demanded obedience. This obedience was to be shown by man keeping God's commandments.

One of the first commandments that God gave man was, *"You may freely eat of every tree of the garden; but of the tree of the knowledge of good and evil you shall not eat, for in the day that you eat of it you shall die"* (Genesis 2:16-17). It was a simple command which could be obeyed. Man had no need to disobey, since God had given him freedom to eat of all the other trees. Man, however, disobeyed; for the Scripture says, *"When the woman saw that the tree was good for food, and that it was a delight to the eyes, and that the tree was to be desired to make one wise, she took of its fruit and ate; and she also gave some to her husband, and he ate"* (Genesis 3:6). This was a wilful act. It was not done in ignorance. Man knew what he was doing. He deliberately decided that he knew better than God and that he wanted independence from God. In that act, man sinned, for sin is choosing one's own way instead of God's way; it is doing that which one knows one should not do and leaving undone what one knows one ought to do.

## THE RESULTS OF ADAM'S SIN

The first result of Adam's sin was that he was no longer comfortable in God's presence. When God came down for His normal fellowship with him, he was nowhere to be found. God called out, *"Where are you?"* (Genesis 3:9), and Adam replied, *"I heard the sound of thee in the garden, and I was afraid, because I was naked; and I hid myself."* (Genesis 3:10) Man was afraid, and he hid himself. His sin brought fear and hiding. He could no longer enjoy God's presence, and fear filled his heart.

The second result was that man was driven out of the garden (God's presence). *"He drove out the man; and at the east gate of the garden of Eden he placed the cherubim, and a flaming sword which turned every way, to guard the way to the tree of life"* (Genesis 3:24).

Being now unfit for a proper relationship with God, Adam was sent away from God's presence and the cherubim and flaming sword put at the gate to ensure that every attempt by man to return to God on his (man's) own conditions is resisted by God and rendered impossible.

The third result of sin was that man died. God had said that man would die the day he disobeyed. That exactly happened on the day Adam sinned. He did not die physically, but he died spiritually. He continued to function biologically, but he was out of touch with God, and this is death. He could no longer talk with God as before, nor could he enjoy God's presence as before. He could not understand God's fullest purpose for his life any more, nor could he fulfil that purpose. He was just there: physically alive but spiritually dead, because he was out of touch with God.

## ALL HAVE SINNED

The Bible says, *"When Adam had lived a hundred and thirty years, he became the father of a son in his own likeness, after his image"* (Genesis 5:3). Adam's children were in his likeness and image. This was not the pure and perfect image of God in which Adam was created. Rather, it was God's image twisted, bent, crooked, distorted and ruined. The image remained God's, but it was God's image in a sad condition, nothing like the original.

All human beings are descendants of Adam, and are born with God's image and likeness in them, twisted and distorted. The twisted image means that they will naturally bend in the direction of sin. Just as a plant will bend in the direction of light (phototropism), man will bend in the direction of sin (sin-tropism).

It is not primarily because a man is a liar, fornicator, thief, idolater, murderer... that he is a sinner. It is basically the fact that his nature, his very being, deep down in him, is sinful. It is as if there is a sin factory in him. Even when the factory is not manufacturing sin because, probably, there are no raw materials, the factory is nevertheless there, very present in every human being. Man is a sinner by nature and his practice of sin is just proof of his nature.

In this matter of a sinful heart, there are no exceptions. The Bible says, *"The Lord saw that the wickedness of man was great in the earth, and that every imagination of the thoughts of his heart was ONLY evil continually"* (Genesis 6:5). *"They are corrupt, they do abominable deeds, there is NONE that does good. The Lord looks down from heaven upon the children of men, to see if there are any that act wisely, that seek after God. They have ALL gone astray, they are ALL alike corrupt; there is NONE that does good, no, not one"* (Psalm 14:1-3); *"We have ALL become like one who is unclean, and ALL our righteous deeds are like polluted garments. We ALL fade like a leaf, and our iniquities, like the wind, take us away. There is NO ONE that calls upon thy name ..."*(Isaiah 64:6-7). *"The heart is deceitful above ALL things, and desperately corrupt; who can understand it?"* (Jeremiah 17:9).

Someone may ask, "Since the above passages are all from the Old Testament, does the New Testament not paint a better picture of man?" The New Testament says, *"NONE IS righteous, no, NOT ONE; NO ONE understands, NO ONE seeks for God. ALL have turned aside, together they have gone wrong; no one does good, not even one. Their throat is an open grave, they use their tongues to deceive"* (Romans 3:10-13). *"ALL have sinned and fall short of the glory of God"* (Romans 3:23).

The Bible insists that all have sinned. The words ALL and NONE tell us who are involved: everybody!! There are no exceptions. A doctor of philosophy and a pupil in primary one are both sinners; a university professor and the most ignorant jungle dweller are both sinners; the richest man and the poorest beggar are both sinners; a pastor or priest and a prostitute are both sinners; a black person and a white person are both sinners. The most cultured man living in the heart of London or New York and the most primitive jungle dweller in the Amazon forests of South America, are both sinners. Education or civilisation does not change the human heart. As far as our sinful nature is concerned, education mainly provides a method of hiding sin and pretending that it is absent. The educated man is a sophisticated sinner. When a primitive man hates you, he immediately tells you so, or the expression on his face tells you. However, the educated man will smile even when hatred boils in his heart. The two hearts are essentially the same.

## SIN IN PRACTICE

If each one of us only had a sin-factory inside him or her that was permanently out of action and, therefore, produced no sins, the situation would be slightly different and we might be tempted to deceive ourselves that the factory is absent. The truth is that the factory is working full-time, even if the productivity may vary from person to person.

What are some of the products from the sin-factories inside us? There are many and can be divided into two classes. First of all, there is what may be hidden inside us which most people cannot see. The root of all of them is independence from God. God is often seen as an interferer. He may be invited to do us some service when we are sick and in need of something, and may be occasionally or regularly asked to go with us to church where we can meet our friends and show off as religious persons. However, when it comes to the details of how we conduct our friendships with the opposite sex, how we acquire and spend our money and all the like, He must keep a distance and not interfere. Then there are sins committed in our thinking, like looking at people lustfully. *"Every one who looks at a woman lustfully has already committed adultery with her in his heart"* (Matthew 5:28). Another is hatred. Most people hate some one or the other and treat this lightly; but the Bible says, *"Any one who hates his brother is a murderer, and you know that no murderer has eternal life abiding in him"* (1 John 3:15). Then there is the main sin of failing to love God *"with all your heart, and with all your soul, and with all your strength, and with all your mind; and your neighbour as yourself"* (Luke 10:27).

Secondly, there are sins that are downright open. These include: *"all manner of wickedness, evil, covetousness, malice, envy, quarrelling, deceit, gossip, insolence, disobedience to parents"* (Romans 1:29-31); *"fornication, idolatry, theft, drunkenness"* (1 Corinthians 6:9-10); *"faithlessness, sorcery, lying"* (Revelation 21:8).

Broken engagements, broken friendships, broken marriages, broken homes, countless children born outside of wedlock, unfaithful husbands, unfaithful wives, corruption at all levels, nepotism, bribery, laziness at work, destruction of property simply because it belongs to the state or some organization, frustration, suicide, murder, and so on, all point to the fact that humanity is very sin-sick.

These are just a few of the sins that people commit. The particular type of sins will vary from person to person. Some might be great liars, others very immoral, others thieves, others full of jealousy, others drunkards, and so on. One does not have to commit all the sins in the catalogue to know that one is a sinner. In fact, when one sin is committed, it immediately shows up the person who commits it for who he is, and the Bible says, *"For whoever keeps the whole law but fails in one point has become guilty of all of it"* (James 2:10).

As you read this catalogue of sins and sinful attitudes, and as you look into your heart and life, do you agree with God's Word that you, as an individual, are a sinner and that you fall short of the glory of God? If you have never committed even one sin, then God is a liar and the rest of this book is useless to you.

## THE WAGES OF SIN

Adam's sin resulted in his separation from God, which is death. Death was the salary he received for sinning. The same applies to all people, for *"the wages of sin is death"* (Romans 6:23). This means that when one sins, one must receive a salary or payment for one's sin. If you are employed by the government or by some other organization and you work faithfully throughout the month, you rightly expect a salary at the end of the month. Something would be wrong with your employer if he did not pay you, and you would rightly deserve to be angry with him.

The salary that sin earns is two-fold. First of all, it is separation from God. As Adam was after he sinned, so man is out of proper touch with God. He does not really know God at a personal level and is very uncomfortable in His presence. He is frustrated and cannot realise his fullest potential. Think of all the people who have been ruined by alcohol, disobedience and selfishness. Think of all the girls who are thrown out of school because of pregnancy. Think of the men with venereal diseases; of the homes that are broken by quarrels, and so on. These are the first instalments of the salary which sin earns for the sinner.

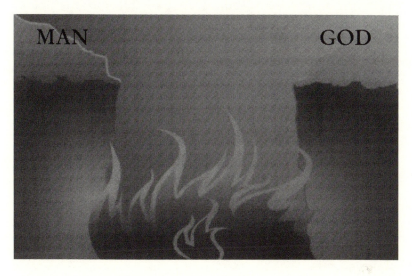

*Adam and God became separated by a big gap when Adam sinned.*
*Man's sin separates him from God*

Secondly, the salary that sin earns is judgment and punishment. Separation is going to last throughout this life and will continue throughout the next. All who are comfortable in their sin and separation from God now, will not be comfortable in the next life, for all human beings will be judged. Some will be sentenced. *"It is appointed for men to die once, and after that comes judgment"* (Hebrews 9:27).

In preparation for the Judgment Day, God is keeping a record of every man's actions. All sins that you commit in thought, word and deed are faithfully recorded against your name in the heavenly record as if in a film. That film of your sins will be projected on a screen on the Judgment Day for you and every other person to see. The things done in darkness will then be shown in the open. Nothing is being left out in the daily recording of your actions, and everything will be projected for you and for all to see. Sentence means that sinners shall be sent away from God's presence to everlasting hell. *"Do you not know that the unrighteous will not inherit the kingdom of God? Do not be deceived; neither fornicators, nor idolaters nor adulterers, nor homosexuals, nor thieves, nor the greedy, nor drunkards, nor revilers, nor robbers will inherit the kingdom of God"* (1 Corinthians 6:9-10). *"But as for the cowardly, the faithless, the polluted, as for murderers, fornicators, sorcerers, idolaters, and all liars, their lot shall be in the lake that burns with fire and sulphur, which is the second death"* (Revelation 21:8). The Judgment Day will be pay day.

Jesus Christ will be the chief Judge: *"The Father judges no one, but has given all judgment to the Son"* (John 5:22). Jesus' words of sentence to unrepentant sinners will be, *"Depart from me, you cursed, into the eternal fire prepared for the devil and his angels"* (Matthew 25:41). These words of judgment will take immediate effect, *"And they will go away into eternal punishment"* (Matthew 25:46).

Hell is a reality that will come into effect after the final judgment, not now. Those who choose to go there will prove its reality in an unchanging personal experience. It is described by

Jesus eleven times in the gospel and He meant business when He said it will be *"everlasting fire"* (Matthew 25:41); *"eternal punishment"* (Matthew 25:46); *"outer darkness"* (Matthew 8:12). The apostle Paul said it will be "eternal destruction" (2 Thessalonians 1:9) and the apostle John said that it will be a *"lake of fire"* (Revelation 19:20).

What all this means is that you, whether you believe it or not, are separated from God and hell-bound, unless you have taken or do now take the right steps to remedy your situation. Hell is your salary for sin, and God will faithfully ensure that no one who has sinned goes without pay. This is very fair. God must punish sin because to do otherwise would be to contradict His nature.

## HUMAN ATTEMPTS AT REACHING GOD

The reality of man's separation from God and the doom of those in hell, has always caused man to attempt to do something about it. The problem is that the gap that separates man from God is a God-gap, and human attempts at bridging it are bound to be unsuccessful. Let us look at some of these attempts at bridging the gap.

Some believe that all you need to do is to be good; to try and maintain a credit balance with God in which the good outweighs the evil. Early in my life I thought so too. This is, of course, unsatisfactory; for God regards human righteousness as filthy rags (Isaiah 64:6). He also regards His law as a whole and those who fail in one part of it fail the whole (James 2:10). Therefore, in God's sight, the one who commits one sin and the one who commits a million sins are both guilty. All who believe in good works are lost, however good they may try to be.

What happens in the recruitment of soldiers illustrates this point clearly. Let us take, for example, that the law of this country demands that only people who are at least five feet and six inches tall, can be recruited into the army. If a man turns up for recruitment and is found by the recruiting officer to be three feet tall, he will be rejected. The same rejection will obviously apply to persons who are four feet five and five feet tall. But what of the person who is five feet five and three quarter inches tall? Does he qualify because he is almost there? No. He, too, is disqualified. He nearly qualified, but did not qualify. He, too, must be rejected.

QUALIFYING LINE------------------------1,80 m

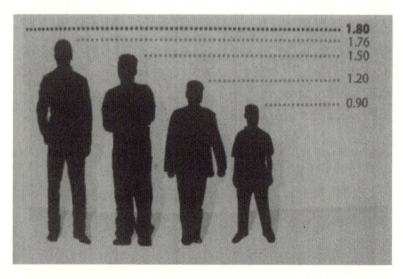

*Although their heights are different, they are, nevertheless, all rejected because they all fall short of the required standard.*

Others believe that all that is needed is a form of religion; so they make up one for themselves or attach themselves to one that was made by man centuries ago. They may fulfil the laws of this man-made religion, but the gap that separates them from God is unaltered.

Others say, all you need to do is to belong to the Christian Church; to be baptized, confirmed and to participate in church life. These things are in themselves not bad. The only problem is that they are the wrong prescription for the disease, "sin". If one baptizes an unrepentant sinner, what does one produce? A baptized sinner! If, later on, the baptized sinner is confirmed, the product is a baptized, confirmed sinner - twice as fit for hell because the external Christian acts have been performed, but the person remains unchanged fundamentally. The gap nevertheless remains. Such people may make some prayer as if through key holes to God; push some money under the door to Him, but they remain separated from Him and their gifts unaccepted, for God cannot accept a man's gifts when the man is himself unaccepted.

*All human attempts at bridging the gap are futile. They all land their masters into the darkness of hell.*

## QUESTIONS

1. What did man have to do so that his relationship with God would continue unhindered?
2. Give a commandment that God gave man at the beginning.
3. How many trees were there in the garden?
4. Of what tree were Adam and Eve not to eat?
5. Did they obey?
6. What is sin? Have you ever sinned?
7. Quote three situations in your life when you chose your own way instead of God's way.
8. What were the results of Adam's sin? (3)
9. How does Adam's sin affect the whole human race? Support your answer with a Bible verse.
10. As you read the catalogue of sins and sinful attitudes, which sins and sinful attitudes do you see
    (a) in your heart?
    (b) in your life?
11. What is the salary received for sinning:
    (a) In time?
    (b) In eternity?
12. What are some of the immediate consequences of sin that you have experienced in your own life?
13. What are some of man's attempts at reaching God?
14. Can baptism and confirmation carried out by some religious systems save a person?
15. Memorise Romans 3:23.

Chapter 3

# THE LOVE
# OF GOD

## GOD'S LOVE FOR THE SINNER

Although God's justice demands that He punishes the sinner eternally, His love for the sinner has always led Him to seek the sinner so that He might bring the sinner back to Himself. The Bible, from the beginning to the end, declares that love. The first words of God to Adam and Eve after they had sinned were, *"Where are you?"* (Genesis 3:9). These words were uttered not because God did not know where they were, but because He wanted them back to Himself. He is a seeking God! When they confessed their nakedness to Him, He made clothing for them out of animal skin (Genesis 3:21). Throughout the Old Testament, by one prophet after the other, He was seeking to reveal Himself to man, to draw man to Himself and to forgive him. He continues to endure the rebellious attitude of man to His invitation to come and be forgiven. It has always been true of Him that, *"The Lord is not slow about his promise as some count slowness, but is forbearing toward you, not wishing that ANY should perish, but that ALL should reach repentance"* (2 Peter 3:9). *"As I live, says the Lord God, I have no pleasure in the death of the wicked, but that the wicked turn from his way and live; turn back, turn back from your evil ways; for why will you die?"* (Ezekiel 33:11).

## GOD'S LOVE REVEALED IN CHRIST

No one can truly love and yet not give to the object of love. God's love for the sinner did not remain as a good feeling. It was revealed in practical terms. *"For God so loved the world that he gave his only Son, that whoever believes in him should not perish but have eternal life"* (John 3:16). *"But God shows his love for us in that while we were yet sinners Christ died for us"* (Romans 5:8). *"In this the love of God was made manifest among us, that God sent his only Son into the world, so that we might live through him"* (1 John 4:9) God gave Christ to die for us. He gave the very best that He had. It must have hurt Him deeply to give His only Son, but love does not spare the best.

## JESUS CHRIST AND HIS MISSION

The Bible tells us that Jesus Christ is the Son of God, (Galatians 2:20). He is one with the Father (John 10:30). God Himself described Him as, *"My beloved Son, with whom I am well pleased"* (Matthew 17:5). Before coming to earth, Jesus Christ always lived in the immediate presence of God and all the glory and honour of heaven were His (John 17:5). He was sent by the Father into the world. *"For God so loved the world that he gave his only Son, that whoever believes in him should not perish but have eternal life"* (John 3:16). He was miraculously born into a human family and grew up like every other child. At the age of thirty, He started His life's work: went everywhere preaching the Good News and healing all kinds of diseases. His mission was to destroy Satan's works; for: "he himself likewise partook of the same nature, that through death he might destroy him who has the power of death, that is, the devil" (Hebrews 2:14). *"The reason the Son of God appeared was to destroy the works of the devil"* (1 John 3:8). Jesus Himself said that He was sent to *"preach good news to the poor... proclaim release to the captives and recovering of sight to the blind, to set at liberty those who are oppressed, to proclaim the acceptable year of the Lord"* (Luke 4:18-19).

Jesus set Himself to deal with the sin problem: the problem of the barrier between man and God. This was the central point of His mission: *"The saying is sure and worthy of full acceptance, that Christ Jesus came into the world to save sinners"* (1 Timothy 1:15). Jesus Himself said, *"...the Son of Man came to seek and to save the lost."* (Luke 19:10). *"I came not to call the righteous, but sinners"* (Mark 2:17). He was out and out to bring the sinner back into the proper relationship with God, such as Adam had before he sinned, so that, like Adam before the fall, there might be unhindered fellowship between man and God.

MAN 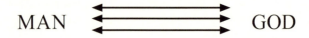 GOD

*Christ's mission was to ensure that the broken relationship between man and God was restored to what it was before sin came in.*

## HOW JESUS DID IT

Jesus carried out His mighty work of saving sinners by dying on the cross. This was absolutely necessary; for: *"without the shedding of blood there is no forgiveness of sins"* (Hebrews 9:22). And Jesus said, *"This is my blood... which is poured out for many for the forgiveness of sins"* (Matthew 26:28). He was not forced to die. His death was rather a personal choice for, long before He was arrested, He said, *"I lay down my life, that I may take it again. No one takes it from me, but I lay it down of my own accord"* (John 10:17-18).

On the cross He died where each sinner ought to have died. He tasted hell on the cross; for from it He cried, *"My God, my God, why hast thou forsaken me?"* (Mark 15:34). Hell will be that place where the eternally lost will cry, "My God, my God, why hast thou forsaken me?" for billions of years, but will receive no answer. God put on Him the sins that every member of the human race ever committed, is committing and will ever commit, and sentenced sin in Him once for all. His death was real. There was no game in it. Its reality was attested by the Roman soldiers who were very experienced at the job. *"But when they came to Jesus and saw that he was already dead, they did not break his legs. But one of the soldiers pierced his side with a spear, and at once there came out blood and water"* (John 19:33-34). After that, He was buried.

Christ's death for sin and for the sinner is sufficient for the release of the sinner and the forgiveness of his sin. *"If the sprinkling of defiled persons with the blood of goats and bulls and with the ashes of a heifer sanctifies for the purification of the flesh, how much more shall the blood of Christ...purify your conscience from dead works to serve the living God"* (Hebrews 9:13-14).

Christ's death on the cross was not only sufficient, it was final.

It can never be repeated and it never will be repeated. *"And by that will we have been sanctified through the offering of the body of Jesus Christ once for all"* (Hebrews 10:10). *"He has appeared ONCE FOR ALL at the end of the age to put away sin by the sacrifice of himself"* (Hebrews 9:26); *"There no longer remains a sacrifice for sins"* (Hebrews 10:26). Jesus Himself said: *"I have finished the work which thou gavest me to do"* (John 17:4), and on the cross He said, *"It is finished"* (John 19:30). The veil in the temple that separated the Holy of Holies from the rest of the temple was torn from top to bottom to demonstrate that the barrier had been done away with permanently.

## WHY JESUS DID IT: LOVE

Although man was lost and needed to be saved, and although the Father wanted him saved, this did not put an obligation on Jesus. All that He did was motivated by love. As the Father so loved the world that He gave His Son for its salvation, so also did Jesus Christ the Son love the world so much that He gave Himself away for its salvation.

In all His teaching, miracles and life, Jesus was love incarnate. He loved the most unlovable, touched the most untouchable and made friends with the rejects of society. Think of the Samaritan woman at the well, who had been rejected by five husbands and was trying it out with a sixth man, when she met Jesus. Each of these men saw her as something to be used and then thrown away. But Jesus saw her as a person, loved her with an all-encompassing love that forgave her sin and gave her a fresh start and a bright future. Think of the woman who was caught in the very act of adultery. Her neighbours judged her and wanted her dead, but Jesus looked at her, loved her and saved her from death by stoning. So mighty was His love for her that it transformed her, an adulteress, into Mary Magdalene the saint. Think of the despised and hated tax collector Zacchaeus, so despised by all for his wicked ways, yet Jesus loved him and paid him a personal visit that led to his repentance and conversion. There is no sinner that Jesus does not love in a personal way. Let me illustrate this with a personal experience. On the 24th of December, 1970, while I was a postgraduate student at Makerere University, Kampala, I wondered how I could best spend the Christmas eve. I later decided to spend the day in prayer and asked the Lord Jesus to send me to people who needed to know the real meaning of Christmas. At seven o'clock that evening, I set out on one of the streets of Kampala telling everyone who was willing to listen to me about the love of Christ. At eleven o'clock as I was returning to the University campus, I stopped by to tell Laban Jumba, who had promised to pray for me, how it had all gone. After a brief chat with him, I began to hurry home as it was rather late. A night watchman stopped me and asked about my identity. I told him who I was and what I had been doing. I further inquired of him if he would let me tell him something about the Lord Jesus. Upon obtaining his permission, I briefly told him about man's need and the love of God as revealed in the life, death and resurrection of Jesus Christ. I further explained to him his own need of repentance towards God and a personal commitment of his life and his all to Christ, for forgiveness and restoration. Upon hearing this, my friend whom I shall call Mr. X, asked me: "Can Jesus receive a wretched sinner like me?" He then went on to tell me the sad story of his life. This is what he said:

"I was a police officer, but when I found that soldiers earned more money and had better privileges than policemen, I resigned from the police force and joined the army. After some time I thought that the best way to make money quickly was to become a businessman. I, therefore, resigned from the army and set up a business. When I began to make money, many women came into my life and each woman took away more money from me than the previous one. Finally, I became broke and my business collapsed. As a penniless man, I decided to seek employment as a night-watchman."

Then he looked at me with tears in his eyes and asked again, "Can Jesus receive a wretched sinner like me?" At that moment, I saw in a new way the glory of the all-loving Christ whose love is so great that He accepts and receives all kinds of repentant sinners, irrespective of the degree of their sin. I gladly told him that Jesus was just too willing to receive him there and then, if he would repent and turn to Him. So we bowed in prayer and Mr. X confessed his sins to God, asked for forgiveness and asked Jesus to come into his life as his Saviour and Lord. He stood up from that prayer a new man, his past sins cancelled and blotted out and his reconciliation to God effected - all these by the grace of God and not by his own merit. *"For by grace you have been saved through faith; and this is not your own doing, it is the gift of God - not because of works, lest any man should boast"* (Ephesians 2:8-9). I kept in touch with him and had the joy of seeing him make progress in his new life with Christ.

Jesus is all-loving. Everything that He did and does for the sinner is motivated by that great love.

## A RISEN CHRIST: GOD'S SEAL ON THE WORK ON THE CROSS

One crucial thing about the death of Christ on the cross is God's evaluation of it. This is because the death on the cross is only as valuable as God saw and sees it. If God thought that it was a failure, then it was a failure. If, on the contrary, He thought it a big success, then it was indeed a success. Was God satisfied with it? Yes, He was! He showed His satisfaction by raising Jesus Christ from the dead on the third day. *"God raised him up"* (Acts 2:24); *"God raised the Lord"* (1 Corinthians 6:14); *"God, who raised him from the dead"* (Colossians 2:12). There is an empty tomb (John 20:1-4), to testify to this.

The raising of Jesus from the dead by God was His stamp of approval on the work on the cross. It was as if God was saying something like this to Christ: "I am perfectly satisfied with your work on the cross on behalf of sinners; I approve of it. Anyone who comes on the basis of what you have done, will be accepted by Me. Rise from the dead and come and sit on My right hand in glory as you did before you went to the world." This stamp of approval by God is irrevocable.

## BENEFITS FROM CHRIST'S DEATH AND RESURRECTION

Jesus Christ's death on the cross accomplished a number of things for the sinner. We shall consider just a few of these.

## JUSTIFICATION

is the rendering of a guilty person before a judge as not guilty. Our sin had made us guilty before God, but through Christ's death on the cross, He made it possible for us to stand before God just as if we had never sinned. *"We are now justified by his blood"* (Romans 5:9). Justification makes it possible for sinners to have peace with God, for: *"Since we are justified by faith, we have peace with God"* (Romans 5:1).

A young man committed a very grievous offence against the law of his country. He was brought before the judge, tried and found guilty. His punishment was stated: death by hanging! As he was about to move towards the place of his death, the judge's only son stepped forward and offered to be punished in the place of this young man. He was stripped and hanged on the tree instead of the young man. The judge's son bore the penalty and the young man was justified. He was asked to go away "just as if he had never committed the offence." He was justified because another took the punishment on his behalf.

Christ did a similar thing. We, like the young man, had sinned very grievously. We had been tried by God, the righteous Judge, and found guilty and our punishment (eternal hell) declared. Jesus, out of love for us, took our place and was hanged on the cross where we ought to have been hanged. In this way, God's demand that sin must be punished was met, and He now says that we may go away as free people who never sinned. This is God's method of setting sinful men free. It is a very costly way, but Jesus paid the price for us. *"The Lord has laid on him the iniquity of us all"* (Isaiah 53:6). *"For Christ also died for sins once for all, the righteous for the unrighteous, that he might bring us to God"* (1 Peter 3:18); and, *"For our sake he made him to be sin who knew no sin, so that in him we might become the righteousness of God"* (2 Corinthians 5:21).

## REDEMPTION

is the setting free through payment of a ransom, of a person who is held in bondage. Sin makes the sinner a prisoner and it has a penalty. By His death on the cross Jesus set the sinner free from both the penalty and power of sin, by paying a price. *"Christ redeemed us from the curse of the law, having become a curse for us"* (Galatians 3:13). *"Jesus Christ, who gave himself for us to redeem us from all iniquity"* (Titus 2:14). *"They are justified by his grace as a gift, through the redemption which is in Christ Jesus"* (Romans 3:24). *"In him we have redemption through his blood, the forgiveness of our trespasses, according to the riches of his grace"* (Ephesians 1:7).

Imagine a slave market. There are slave owners with chained slaves. These slaves are to be sold to some far off country. They are in chains and cannot set themselves free. Suddenly, a big boss comes into the market, pays the price for each slave, takes away the chains and the marks inflicted by the chains, and declares the slaves free. How wonderful! Jesus did just that.

We were Satan's slaves and imprisoned by him, and we were meant to share his home (hell) with him. On the cross, Jesus paid the price for our liberation and now declares us free. The freed slave requires a new home. Jesus also made provision for this by His death on the cross. He first lifted us out of the kingdom of our former master (Satan) and placed us into an entirely new Kingdom, which is His. *"He has delivered us from the dominion of darkness and transferred us to the kingdom of his beloved Son, in whom we have redemption, the forgiveness of sins"* (Colossians 1:13-14).

The story is told of a young man who fell into a pit. Many people passed by and, in order to be safe, stood at a comfortable distance from the pit. From that distance, they began to try and sympathise with him. Some made suggestions to him on how he might get himself out of the pit. One person said to him, "Believe that there is one God and you will be out of the pit." The man in the pit replied that he had never doubted the fact that there is one God. He further said that he believed that absolutely. That, however, did not get him out of the pit. Another person told him that all that was required to get him out of the pit, was for him to fast and pray many times a day. He tried to pray and since there was no food in the pit, fasting posed no problem to him. This also failed to get him out. The third person suggested that he needed to attend church services in a particular denominational church and pay all his subscriptions, and all would be well. He replied that he did, in fact, belong to that denomination and was a financial member in the said church, but since he was in the pit, he needed to get out of it in order to be able to attend church services and bring his financial position in the church up to date. The next man advising him asked, "Are you sure that you are baptized and confirmed? This is all important for getting you out of the pit." He replied that he was fully baptized and confirmed and that his Christian name was John, and that before falling into the pit, he partook of the Holy Communion regularly. He then added with deep frustration, "But all this does not seem to be able to get me out of this pit." Finally, someone great and noble came along. He went very close to the pit and saw the fallen man's plight. He took off his clothing and wore rags and, entering the pit, lifted the fallen man out of it. In the process of lifting him out, he bruised himself and blood flowed out. Outside the pit, he took the dirty clothes off the fallen man and put on him his own rich clothing, saying to the man, "I can get others for myself." Jesus did just that. We had all fallen into "the pit of sin." All human philosophical and religious attempts at getting us out had failed. Seeing our helplessness, Jesus came right into our situation. He unrobed Himself of all His heavenly glory and took upon Himself our humanity, that He might get us out of our mess of sin and clothe us with His glory.

The need for a personal experience of the Lord Jesus as personal Saviour is further borne out by the following testimony of a young lady. She says, "I was born into a religious family, my father being a church minister. In infancy, I was duly baptized and when I became of age, I was confirmed. I dutifully attended Sunday School classes and had nothing against God or Jesus Christ. In fact, I loved God in a vague kind of way, although I did not know Him! While in secondary school, I was an active member of the Student Christian Movement and maintained a high moral standard. After secondary school, I got myself well grounded in church going, and even joined the choir and the Christian Youth group, where I was elected a committee member. In the group, we carried out, among other things, hospital and prison visitation, and I took an active part in these activities. Church going had become such an integral part of my being that I felt ill whenever I could not go to church for one reason or the other. Even after dancing until the early hours of Sunday morning, I always managed to go to church, even though this meant that at times I slept throughout most of the service. With such involvement and zeal in Christian things and not knowing that there was something more in the Christian life, I thought myself a very good Christian. Some of my friends even thought that I was getting too involved with God. This state of things continued until I left the country and went abroad to study. There I joined the Christian Union as usual. I was, however, surprised that the members of this union talked and lived as if Jesus was everything to them. They even claimed to know Him personally. I would have rejected their claims as presumptuous had it not been for the fact that their lives showed that they possessed something positive which I lacked, which they attributed to the inner working of Jesus in their lives. As I continued in that union, I was shown my need of a personal relationship with Jesus Christ. I then repented of all the sins that I could remember to have committed against God and man, then turned my heart and life to Jesus Christ and begged Him to come and live in me. He did come into my heart and life, and my life and christian involvement then took on a new dimension. These activities were now done as an outflow of my new life in Christ. It is nine years since I first came into this life-giving experience with Christ, and I continue to rejoice in Him as my Saviour and Lord."

## RECONCILIATION

is the making of peace between enemies. As a result of our sin, we were at enmity with God, but Christ's death on the cross healed that enmity. The Bible says, *"While we were still weak, at the right time Christ died for the ungodly. Why, one will hardly die for a righteous man - though perhaps for a good man one will dare even to die. But God shows his love for us in that while we were yet sinners Christ died for us"* (Romans 5:6-8). *"While we were enemies we were reconciled to God by the death of his Son"* (Romans 5:10). *"...God,who through Christ reconciled us to himself"* (2 Corinthians 5:18). *"But now in Christ Jesus you who once were far off have been brought near in the blood of Christ"* (Ephesians 2:13); *"...for through him we both have access in one Spirit to the Father"* (Ephesians 2:18).

*The barrier between man and God was bridged by the Cross.*

## ADOPTION

The freed slave does not only need a new home. He needs a new status. Christ's death on the cross also made provision for this. The process is called adoption - a process in which the full rights of a son are conferred on someone who is not one's son by birth. *"When we were children, we were slaves to the elemental spirits of the universe. But when the time had fully come, God sent forth his Son... to redeem those who were under the law, so that we might receive adoption as sons"* (Galatians 4:3-6). *"You have received the spirit of sonship...the Spirit himself bearing witness with our spirit that we are the children of God, and if children, then heirs, heirs of God and fellow heirs with Christ"* (Romans 8:15-17).

By Christ's death on the cross this possibility of becoming God's child is open to everyone in general and to you in particular. You can indeed become a child of God and enjoy all the rights of a son, even to the extent of sharing the throne of God with Jesus Christ, God's begotten Son. *"But to all who received him, who believed in his name, he gave the power to become the children of God"* (John 1:12).

## QUESTIONS

1. What is God's will for every sinner?
2. How did God show His love for the sinner?
3. Give two reasons why Jesus came into the world. Use Bible verses in your answer.
4. How did Jesus carry out His work of saving sinners?
5. Was Christ forced to die?
6. Do you know one particular person for whom Christ died on the Cross?
7. Give one Bible verse that says that Christ's sacrifice on the Cross was final and that henceforth no other sacrifice was necessary.
8. Since Jesus was not forced to die, what moved Him to die on the Cross for the salvation of sinners?
9. Is there a sinner who has sinned so much that Jesus would not receive him?
10. What did God do to show that He was satisfied with Christ's work on the Cross?
11. Say in your own words what justification means.
12. How are we justified?
13. What is redemption? What did Christ do to redeem the sinner?
14. Look again at the story of the young man who fell into a pit. Five people tried to help him out. Which of them represents the Lord Jesus? Explain.

15. What is reconciliation? Why do you as a sinner need to be reconciled to God?
16. What is adoption? Is it possible for a sinner to become a child of God? How?
17. Memorise John 3:16 and Isaiah 53:6.

Chapter 4

# GOD FORGIVES YOU

## WHAT YOU MUST DO

God in Christ has done everything that is necessary for the sinner to be forgiven. The only thing that is left is the sinner's response. This is important because God's forgiveness, which is based on Christ's death and resurrection, is only effective for those who respond rightly. You must respond, first of all, because you do not want to treat all that Christ did for you lightly. You want to be grateful. Secondly, because you need forgiveness for all the sins that you have committed and you want the penalty of your sins to be cancelled. Thirdly, because you need Christ to live the type of life that God wants you to live.

There are some things you should do to be forgiven.

**The first is:**

ADMIT that you are a sinner. Tell God that you have personally sinned in your actions, in your words and in your thoughts. Tell Him all the sins you remember to have committed against Him, and against any other person. Be specific. If you stole, tell Him what you stole and from whom you stole it. If you were immoral, tell Him with whom you committed the immorality. If you lied, tell Him all the lies you can remember. Take your time about this, even if it lasts for many hours. Do not leave out any sin that you remember and do not try to hide some, for *"he who conceals his transgressions will not prosper, but he who confesses and forsakes them will obtain mercy"* (Proverbs 28:13). Tell God that you are sorry for your sins, and ask Him to forgive you. *"Godly grief produces a repentance that leads to salvation and brings no regret, but worldly grief produces death"* (2 Corinthians 7:10).

If you are truly sorry for your sins, you will determine to put them away - to stop sinning. *"Let the wicked forsake his way, and the unrighteous man his thoughts; let him return to the Lord, that he may have mercy on him, and to our God, for he will abundantly pardon"* (Isaiah 55:7). You may have to return the things you stole or, at least, confess to the people involved that you stole their things. You will have to put some of the chaos caused by your past life in order. This is costly and may make you look small before some people, but all the same, do it. Christ will give you a new reputation and, after all, the most important thing is God's opinion of you and not that of man.

**The second thing is:**

BELIEVE that Christ died for you. This means that with your whole heart, mind and all, you believe that Jesus Christ actually died on the cross for the whole world and for you as an individual. In believing this you are saying that all attempts to get to heaven by good works and keeping the commandments are useless. *"No human being will be justified in his sight by works of the law"* (Romans 3:20). In believing that Christ died for you, you are also saying that He is the only One who can forgive sins and restore you to a proper relationship with God, and that any other person or any other system that claims to do the same is completely mistaken and very wrong. *"And there is salvation in no one else, for there is no other name under heaven given among men by which we must be saved"* (Acts 4:12). *"There is one God, and there is one mediator between God and men, the man Christ Jesus"* (1 Timothy 2:5). Jesus Himself said, *"I am the way, and the truth, and the life; no one comes to the Father, but by me"* (John 14:6). Finally, in believing that Christ died for you, you are duty bound to live for Him. *"He died for all, that those who live might live NO LONGER FOR THEMSELVES BUT FOR HIM who for their sake died and was raised"* (2 Corinthians 5:15). This means that you are prepared to surrender yourself to him completely, holding nothing back, since He did not hold anything back, but gave His whole self for you on the cross. Think seriously about this and count the cost.

**The third thing is:**

COME to Him and make Him your Saviour and Lord. He died for you and rose again. Now, you respond to His death and resurrection. Receive Him. *"To all who received Him... he gave power to become children of God"* (John 1:12). Jesus Christ said, *"Behold, I stand at the door, and knock; if any one hears my voice and opens the door, I will come in to him"* (Revelation 3:20). He is knocking at your door. All that you have been reading in this book is a message to you from Him. He wants you to open the "door" of your heart and life and to receive Him. He is knocking right now.

## A TIME FOR ACTION

Do not postpone receiving Him. Act now. It is urgent. *"Behold now is the acceptable time; behold, now is the day of salvation"* (2 Corinthians 6:2) *"Today, when you hear his voice, do not harden your hearts"* (Hebrews 3:15). The invitation is urgent. Jesus is waiting and says, *"Come to me...and I will give you rest"* (Matthew 11:28). Do not put it off until the evening or tomorrow. There are a number of reasons why putting off the decision until another time is very unwise. The first is that God has said, TODAY. If you say, "tomorrow", you are either saying that God is wrong or that you are foolish. The second is that God may give you up. God gives up people who do not want to act on the truth they know (Romans 1:18-20), and He hardens the hearts of those who initially harden their hearts against Him. Thirdly, death may come upon you suddenly. You are not too young or too old to die. You can be taken by surprise. Are you prepared to meet God as you are? To postpone is to reject Him. So you should act now!!!

## RECEIVING CHRIST

You can receive Him by simply telling Him in prayer to come into your heart and life. Below is a suggested prayer inviting Jesus into a life. If you want Him to come into your life right now, you should pray in the following words or in words of your own, and Jesus will come into your heart.

"Lord Jesus, I (MR./MRS/MISS/DR/REV/EL HADJ..

have personally sinned against You in my thoughts, in my words and in my actions. Nothing that I can do on my own can take away my sin. I deserve to go to hell. But You died for a helpless sinner like me so that I can be forgiven. I surrender myself to You completely, holding nothing back. Take away all my sins and come into my heart by Your Holy Spirit as my own Saviour and Lord, and do with my life as You desire. I will follow You at any cost. Thank You for hearing my prayer and coming into my heart. Amen."

If you have prayed this prayer very sincerely, then Jesus has, straight away, come to live in you by His Holy Spirit.

## QUESTIONS

1. Since Christ died on the Cross for all sinners, are all sinners therefore automatically forgiven, saved?
2. Explain simply the four steps that a sinner must follow in order to be forgiven.
3. Do you want to be forgiven?
4. Have you decided to stop sinning?
5. Have you done what you must do to receive God's forgiveness.
6. Give one important reason why you must not postpone your decision to receive God's forgiveness, why you must receive Christ today.
7. How can a sinner receive the Lord Jesus? Have you personally received Christ?
8. Memorise John 1:12.

Chapter 5

# BECAUSE YOU ARE FORGIVEN

You are NOW forgiven by God. He has taken away your sins completely. He says, *"If we confess our sins, he is faithful and just, and will forgive us our sins and cleanse us from ALL unrighteousness"* (1 John 1:9). He has done just that for you who have received Him. He has not only forgiven you. He has forgotten! What a wonderful God!! He says; *"I will remember their sins and their misdeeds NO MORE"* (Hebrews 10:17). And again, *"Thou wilt cast ALL our sins into the depths of the sea"* (Micah 7:19). There is no more condemnation for you (Romans 8:1). Your record of sins is cancelled forthwith, and the film destroyed permanently. You are now the object of God's special love and favour. Do not depend on your feelings. Depend on the promises of the God who cannot lie, for *"God is not man, that he should lie"* (Numbers 23:19). If in future you commit any sin, just turn immediately to the Saviour who lives in you and ask for forgiveness. You are now His child. He will never get tired of forgiving you. Only do not sin deliberately.

## ETERNAL LIFE

Because you are now forgiven, you have eternal life. It has indeed begun for you and will continue in heaven. The apostle John, in writing about this, says, *"God gave us eternal life, and this life is in his Son. He who has the Son has life; he who has not the Son of God has not life. I write this to you who believe in the name of the Son of God, that you may KNOW that you have eternal life"* (1 John 5:11-13). Jesus also said, *"My sheep hear my voice, and I know them, and they follow me; and I give them eternal life, and they shall never perish, and no one shall snatch them out of my hand"* (John 10:27-28). *"For the wages of sin is death, but the free gift of God is eternal life in Christ Jesus our Lord"* (Romans 6:23).

## ETERNAL SECURITY

Because you are now forgiven, you will not lose your salvation. God's forgiveness is not for a few seconds or days or years. It is for ever. You have been born into God's family, and you shall no more be born out of it. God is going to guard the life He has given you, cause it to grow and flourish, and keep it safe. Jesus says, *"My sheep hear my voice, and I know them, and they follow me; and I give them eternal life, and they shall never perish, and NO ONE shall snatch them out of my hand. My Father, who has given them to me, is greater than all, and NO ONE is able to snatch them out of the Father's hand. I and the Father are one"* (John 10:27-30). So you have a three-fold security: the Holy Spirit in you, Jesus' hand around you, and God the Father's hand around the hand of Jesus. What security!! Keep hearing His voice and keep following Him, and your eternal life is guaranteed. Do not abuse this guarantee by going back to your sinful ways. You have become a new creature in Christ. Let the way you live reflect this.

Very recently, I bought a car. The young man who went with me to show me where the registration is done asked me to declare a lower price than what I had paid for it, so that I would pay a much lower registration tax. I told him that such an action would be wrong. He replied that I would be cheating no one but the government, and that every one cheats the government whenever it can safely be done. I finally told him that whether or not everybody did it, did not make it a right action, and I was not going to follow suit. He then said to me, "You are the biggest fool I have met in this country, a fool who is willing to throw away money." This is part of being a new creature in Christ with an eternal security, that is, to be honest at all times, even if it means that we are called "biggest fools." Be prepared to be a "fool" for Christ. His "fools" are wonderful. *"For the foolishness of God is wiser than men, and the weakness of God is stronger than men"* (1 Corinthians 1:25).

## HEAVENLY CITIZENSHIP

Because you are now forgiven; you have been transferred from the devil's kingdom into the Kingdom of Christ (Colossians 1:13-14). You are now a citizen of heaven (Hebrews 13:14). You may be wondering how a very unworthy person like you can receive the full citizenship of heaven. You may feel that you do not deserve it. You are right in feeling unworthy and undeserving, but, nevertheless, your heavenly citizenship is your present standing as a forgiven sinner. Let me illustrate this with a true story.

Many years ago, in the colonial era, when every white person was a dignitary, an important football match was to take place at Kampala. All important personalities were invited. A certain missionary, as a white dignitary, was given a special V.I.P. pass to the match, but owing to pressing duties, he gave his pass to one of his primary school teachers to attend the match in his place. When the teacher got to the stadium, by the looks of his unimpressive clothing, he was asked to go away. When he insisted and said that he had a ticket, he was asked to go to the open stand where people with the cheapest tickets stood. On his way to that stand he met another police officer who did not look at his appearance but at his ticket. On seeing that he had a V.I.P. pass, he said to him, "You are for that comfortable stand there. Your ticket indicates that." So this poorly dressed man went to that stand and, as he showed his ticket to the police officers in attendance, he was asked to go higher and higher up the stairs until he got to the topmost one, and found himself next to the famous king of Buganda and the colonial governor of Uganda. On his own merit he deserved nothing, but by virtue of the pass that he received undeservedly, he was given a place of the highest honour.

At the moment you receive Jesus Christ as your personal Saviour, even though you have no personal merits of your own, God, however, confers upon you spiritual greatness. He gives you heavenly citizenship free of charge, makes you His ambassador on earth with special diplomatic status and duties, and at death gives you a ticket to all the banquets in heaven. All these honours are yours because of your special relationship to Jesus Christ.

## TELL OTHERS

Jesus told the people he healed to go home and tell others. *"Go home to your friends, and tell them how much the Lord has done for you, and how he has had mercy on you"* (Mark 5:19). He was obeyed, for in one instance, we are told that the man who was healed *"went away and began to proclaim in the Decapolis how much Jesus had done for him; and all men marvelled"* (Mark 5:20). You, too, have been healed of the disease of sin and forgiven by God. Because you are now forgiven, go and tell others: your family members, your friends and everybody. BEGIN TODAY. Some will laugh at you; others will persecute you, but go on. After all, they did the same to your Saviour and what they did to the Master, they will do to the servant. Let them see by the way you talk and act that what you are saying is true.

## PRAY EVERY DAY

Because you are now forgiven and made a child of God, you can talk directly to God. He is now your Father. There is no longer a barrier between you and Him. Make a special time when you can really talk to Him, telling Him how you love Him and how grateful you are to Him for saving you. Ask Him for ANYTHING you need and put the needs of your family, friends and enemies before Him. Just be free with Him and tell Him anything and everything. He says*, "Truly, truly, I say unto you, if you ask anything of the Father, he will give it to you in my name"* (John 16:23). Sometimes, just stay quiet before

Him and He will speak to your heart. You can also talk to Him at any place and at any time, in a bus, on the field, in bed, in the morning, at noon, at midnight - anytime, anywhere. He will never be tired of listening to you. He desires to hear you talk to Him. It pleases Him.

## READ THE BIBLE EVERY DAY

The Bible is God's Word to you. Because you are forgiven, read it prayerfully every day. Also set a special time for doing so: maybe just before or just after your special time of prayer. Begin with St. John's gospel and read it from start to finish. Go as quickly as possible and read the whole New Testament twice in the next six months. Have a note book in which you write out what God is saying to you, and some verses which you have memorised. The Bible will keep you away from sin, but sin will also try to keep you away from it. Do not give in to Satan, but resist him and he will flee from you. (James 4 : 7-8).

## FINALLY

Finally, press on with the Lord at all costs. Do not give up, even if you are persecuted. Remember that, *"It has been granted to you that for the sake of Christ you should not only believe in him but also suffer for his sake"* (Philippians 1:29). This suffering will be rewarded. Jesus is preparing a wonderful place for you in heaven, and as a reward for your faithfulness, you will sit on the throne with Him.

## QUESTIONS

Are your sins forgiven? Support your answer with Bible verses.

1. What is eternal life?
2. Do you have eternal life? How do you know? (Use a Bible verse).
3. When did eternal life begin in you?
4. How can someone who is a Cameroonian also become a citizen of heaven?
5. Name one responsibility of someone whose sins are forgiven.
6. What must you do to strengthen your new life? (Two things).
7. Memorise 1 John 5:11 – 13.

# THANK YOU FOR READING THIS BOOK

If you have any question and/or need help, do not hesitate to contact us through **ztfbooks@cmfionline.org**. If the book has blessed you, then we would also be grateful if you leave a positive review at your favorite (online) retailer.

**ZTF BOOKS, through Christian Publishing House (CPH)** offers a wide selection of best selling Christian books (in print-POD, eBook & audiobook formats) on a broad spectrum of topics, including marriage & family, sexuality, practical spiritual warfare, Christian service, Christian leadership, and much more. Visit us at **www.ztfbooks.com** to learn more about our latest releases and special offers. **And thank you for being a ZTF BOOK reader.**

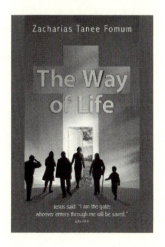

We would like to recommend to you the first book in The Christian Way Series - The Way of Life:

*This book, "The Way of Life," being the first book in the series, has as its theme, the Way into the Christian Life - the Way into Jesus Christ - the Way into God - the Way of Life.*

*It is written specially to help you*

*to find the Lord Jesus, give yourself to Him, and then you will truly begin to live. As you begin to read, we encourage you to press on right to the end and also answer all the questions at the end of each chapter.*

*Our prayer is that, by the time you finish reading it, you will have entered into a living relationship with Jesus and then you, too, can say, "Jesus is my Saviour."*

*May God bless you very richly!*

*Thank you and God bless you!*

Zacharias Tanee Fomum

# CONNECT WITH THE AUTHOR

• **Social media: Facebook**, **Twitter**, **YouTube**, **Instagram**

**website:** http://www.cmfionline.org

**Order print copies:** http://www.cph.cmfionline.org

**FREE online Bible Course:** http://www.bcc.cmfionline.org

**Internet Radio:** https://cmfiradio.org

**Podcast:** https://soundcloud.com/rvcast

We equally offer training courses (all year round) from basic to university level at the **University of Prayer and Fasting** (WUPF) and the **School of Knowing and Serving God** (SKSG). You are highly welcome to enroll at your soonest convenience. Or maybe **our online course** will be much handy?

# VERY IMPORTANT!!!

If you have not yet received Jesus as your Lord and Saviour, I encourage you to receive Him. Here are some steps to help you,

**ADMIT** that you are a sinner by nature and by practice and that on your own you are without hope. Tell God you have personally sinned against Him in your thoughts, words and deeds. Confess your sins to Him, one after another in a sincere prayer. Do not leave out any sins that you can remember. Truly turn from your sinful ways and abandon them. If you stole, steal no more. If you have been committing adultery or fornication, stop it. God will not forgive you if you have no desire to stop sinning in all areas of your life, but if you are sincere, He will give you the power to stop sinning.

**BELIEVE** that Jesus Christ, who is God's Son, is the only Way, the only Truth and the only Life. Jesus said, "I am the way, the truth and the life; no one comes to the Father, but by me" (John 14:6). The Bible says, "For there is one God, and there is one mediator between God and men, the man Christ Jesus, who gave himself as a ransom for all" (1 Timothy 2:5-6). "And there is salvation in no one else (apart from Jesus), for there is no other name under heaven given among men by which we must be saved" (Acts 4:12). But to all who received him, who believed in his name, he gave power to become children of God..." (John 1:12). BUT,

**CONSIDER** the cost of following Him. Jesus said that all who follow Him must deny themselves, and this includes selfish financial, social and other interests. He also wants His followers to take up their crosses and follow Him. Are you prepared to abandon your own interests daily for those of Christ? Are you prepared to be led in a new direction by Him? Are you prepared to suffer for Him and die for Him if need be? Jesus will have nothing to do with half-hearted people. His demands are total. He will only receive and forgive those who are prepared to follow Him AT ANY COST. Think about it and count the cost. If you are prepared to follow Him, come what may, then there is something to do.

**INVITE** Jesus to come into your heart and life. He says, "Behold I stand at the door and knock. If anyone hears my voice and opens the door (to his heart and life), I will come in to him and eat with him, and he with me " (Revelation 3:20). Why don't you pray a prayer like the following one or one of your own construction as the Holy Spirit leads?

> *"Lord Jesus, I am a wretched, lost sinner who has sinned in thought, word and deed. Forgive all my sins and cleanse me. Receive me, Saviour and transform me into a child of God. Come into my heart now and give me eternal life right now. I will follow you at all costs, trusting the Holy Spirit to give me all the power I need."*

When you pray this prayer sincerely, Jesus answers at once and justifies you before God and makes you His child.

*Please write to me (**ztfbooks@cmfionline.org**) and I will pray for you and help you as you go on with Jesus Christ.*

# OTHER BOOKS FROM THE AUTHOR

## THE CHRISTIAN WAY SERIES

1. The Way Of Life
2. The Way Of Obedience
3. The Way Of Discipleship
4. The Way Of Sanctification
5. The Way Of Christian Character
6. The Way Of Spiritual Power
7. The Way Of Christian Service
8. The Way Of Spiritual Warfare
9. The Way Of Suffering For Christ
10. The Way Of Victorious Praying
11. The Way Of Overcomers
12. The Way Of Spiritual Encouragement
13. The Way Of Loving The Lord

## THE PRAYER POWER SERIES

1. The Way Of Victorious Praying
2. The Ministry Of Fasting
3. The Art Of Intercession
4. The Practice Of Intercession
5. Praying With Power
6. Practical Spiritual Warfare Through Prayer
7. Moving God Through Prayer
8. The Ministry Of Praise And Thanksgiving
9. Waiting On The Lord In Prayer
10. The Ministry Of Supplication
11. Life-Changing Thoughts On Prayer, Volume 1
12. The Centrality Of Prayer
13. Spiritual Aggressiveness
14. Life-Changing Thoughts On Prayer, Volume 2
15. Prayer and Spiritual Intimacy
16. Life-Changing Thoughts on Prayer Volume 3
17. The Art of Worship

## THE PRACTICAL HELPS FOR OVERCOMERS SERIES

1. Discipleship at any cost
2. The Use Of Time
3. Retreats For Spiritual Progress
4. Personal Spiritual Revival
5. Daily Dynamic Encounters With God
6. The School Of Truth
7. How To Succeed In The Christian Life
8. The Christian And Money
9. Deliverance From The Sin Of Laziness
10. The Art Of Working Hard
11. Knowing God - The Greatest Need Of The Hour
12. Revelation: A Must
13. True Repentance
14. Restitution - An Important Message For The Overcomers
15. You Can Receive A Pure Heart Today
16. You Can Lead Someone To The Lord Jesus Today
17. You Can Receive The Baptism Into The Holy Spirit Now
18. The Dignity Of Manual Labour
19. You Have A Talent!
20. The Making Of Disciples
21. The Secret Of Spiritual Fruitfulness
22. Are You Still A Disciple Of The Lord Jesus?
23. The Overcomer As A Servant Of Man

## THE GOD, SEX AND YOU SERIES

1. Enjoying The Premarital Life
2. Enjoying The Choice Of Your Marriage Partner

# OTHER BOOKS FROM THE AUTHOR

3. Enjoying The Married Life
4. Divorce And Remarriage
5. A Successful Marriage; The Husband's Making
6. A Successful Marriage; The Wife's Making

## THE ZTF NEW BOOKS SERIES

1. Power For Service
2. The Art Of Worship
3. Issues Of The Heart
4. In The Crucible For Service
5. Spiritual Nobility
6. Roots And Destinies
7. Revolutionary Thoughts On Spiritual Leadership
8. The Leader And His God
9. The Overthrow Of Principalities And Powers
10. Walking With God
11. God Centeredness
12. Victorious Dispositions
13. The Believer's Conscience
14. The Processes Of Faith
15. Spiritual Gifts
16. The Missionary As A Son
17. You, Your Team And Your Ministry
18. Prayer And A Walk With God
19. Leading A Local Church
20. Church Planting Strategies
21. The Character And The Personality of The Leader
22. Deliverance From The Sin of Gluttony
23. The Spirit Filled Life
24. The Church: Rights And Responsibilities Of The Believer
25. Thoughts On Marriage
26. Learning To Importune In Prayer
27. Jesus Saves And Heals Today
28. God, Money And You
29. Meet The Liberator
30. Salvation And Soul Winning
31. The Salvation Of The Lord Jesus: Soul Winning (Vol. 3)
32. Soul Winning And The Making Of Disciples
33. Victorious Soul Winning
34. Making Spiritual Progress (Vol. 4)
35. Life Changing Thought On Prayer (Vol. 3)
36. Knowing God And Walking With Him
37. What Our Ministry Is
38. Practical Dying To Self And The Spirit-filled Life
39. Leading God's People
40. Laws Of Spiritual Leadership
41. From His Lips: Compilation of Autobiographical Notes on Professor Zacharias Tanee Fomum
42. The School of Soul Winners and Soul Winning
43. The Complete Work of Zacharias Tanee Fomum on Prayer (Volume 1)
44. Knowing and Serving God (Volume 2)
45. Walking With God (Volume 1)

## THE PRACTICAL HELPS IN SANCTIFICATION SERIES

1. Deliverance From Sin
2. The Way Of Sanctification
3. Sanctified And Consecrated For Spiritual Ministry
4. The Sower, The Seed And The Hearts Of Men
5. Freedom From The Sin Of Adultery And Fornication
6. The Sin Before You May Lead To Immediate Death: Do Not Commit It!
7. Be Filled With The Holy Spirit
8. The Power Of The Holy Spirit In The Winning Of The Lost

## THE MAKING SPIRITUAL PROGRESS SERIES

1. Vision, Burden, Action
2. The Ministers And The Ministry of The New Covenant
3. The Cross In The Life And Ministry Of The Believer
4. Knowing The God Of Unparalleled Goodness
5. Brokenness: The Secret Of Spiritual

Overflow
6. The Secret Of Spiritual Rest
7. Making Spiritual Progress, Volume 1
8. Making Spiritual Progress, Volume 2
9. Making Spiritual Progress, Volume 3
10. Making Spiritual Progress, Volume 4

## THE EVANGELISM SERIES

1. God's Love And Forgiveness
2. The Way Of Life
3. Come Back Home My Son; I Still Love You
4. Jesus Loves You And Wants To Heal You
5. Come And See; Jesus Has Not Changed!
6. 36 Reasons For Winning The Lost To Christ
7. Soul Winning, Volume 1
8. Soul Winning, Volume 2
9. Celebrity A Mask

## THE OTHER BOOKS SERIES

1. Laws Of Spiritual Success, Volume 1
2. The Shepherd And The Flock
3. Deliverance From Demons
4. Inner Healing
5. No Failure Needs To Be Final
6. Facing Life's Problems Victoriously
7. A Word To The Students
8. The Prophecy Of The Overthrow Of The Satanic Prince Of Cameroon
9. Basic Christian Leadership
10. A Missionary life and a missionary heart
11. Power to perform miracles

## THE WOMEN OF THE GLORY SERIES

1. The Secluded Worshipper: The Life, Ministry, And Glorification Of The Prophetess Anna
2. Unending Intimacy: The Transformation, Choices And Overflow of Mary of Bethany
3. Winning Love: The rescue, development and fulfilment of Mary Magdalene
4. Not Meant for Defeat: The Rise, Battles, and Triumph of Queen Esther

## THE ANTHOLOGY SERIES

1. The School of Soul Winners and Soul Winning
2. The Complete Works of Zacharias Tanee Fomum on Prayer (Volume 1)
3. The Complete Works of Zacharias Tanee Fomum on Leadership (Volume 1)
4. The Complete Works of Z.T Fomum on Marriage
5. Making Spiritual Progress (The Complete Box Set of Four Volumes)

## THE OTHER BOOKS SERIES

1. A Broken Vessel
2. The Joy of Begging to Belong to the Lord Jesus Christ: A Testimony

## THE BIOGRAPHICAL SERIES

1. From His Lips: ZT Fomum - About himself
2. From His Lips: ZT Fomum - About His Co-Workers
3. From His Lips: ZT Fomum - About His Missions
4. From His Lips: ZT Fomum - About His Work
5. From His Lips: Z.T. Fomum - School of Knowing & Serving God

Manufactured by Amazon.ca
Bolton, ON